African American Brother

African American Brother

TERESA Y. TAYLOR

Epic
Press

Belleville, Ontario, Canada

DEAR AFRICAN AMERICAN BROTHER
Copyright © 2010, Teresa Y. Taylor

ISBN: 978-1-55452-529-4
LSI Edition: 978-1-55452-530-0

To order additional copies, visit:
www.essencebookstore.com

For more information, please contact:
Teresa Y. Taylor
taylorteresa@ymail.com

Epic Press is an imprint of *Essence Publishing,* a Christian Book
Publisher dedicated to furthering the work of Christ through the written
word. For more information, contact:
20 Hanna Court, Belleville, Ontario, Canada K8P 5J2
Phone: 1-800-238-6376 • Fax: (613) 962-3055
E-mail: info@essence-publishing.com
Web site: www.essence-publishing.com

Printed in Canada
by
Epic
Press

Dedication

This book is dedicated to my three daughters, Latoya, Timithia and Tamara. At one point in my life I didn't think I could go on, but when I would think of my girls, I was able to pull myself together and reach a little higher.

I would like to dedicate this book to my niece Shaton and nephews Michael and Daniel. I would also like to thank my daughters' father, Timothy Taylor, for being a wonderful father. There was never a time that my daughters went without food, shoes, clothes and dedication. I am truly grateful that my daughters have him as a father. And lastly, I would like to thank my parents, Acher and Annie Yarbrough, for raising me to believe that there is hope for relationship. After forty-nine years of marriage, two children and six grandchildren, I believe.

Dear African American Brother...

Dear African American Brother,

I saw you standing on the street corner, and I thought you might need a ride. But as I approached you in my car, you held both your hands up asking me to just let you walk across the street. As I looked in your eyes, I could tell that you had other things on your mind. I felt the emptiness as you walked away, but I just couldn't bring myself to say anything. I just had to let you know that I had your back even if you walked on as if I didn't exist. I couldn't see why you were in such a hurry because, when I drove around the corner, you had disappeared. I tried looking for you, but I couldn't find you. I stopped to ask one of your friends about you, but his response was hesitant. He finally told me in street language that you were waiting for the mailman. I couldn't understand that at first, but now I do. I realize that that letter didn't need a stamp.

Since that day, I have been thinking about you. I wanted to remind you of the struggles of your inspiring brothers. I know you have forgotten the hardship your brothers suffered, so I'm going to try and help you remember.

History tells us that your brothers were active and very aggressive in their walk to victory.

You might remember your brother Richard Wright. Richard grew up very poor. He lived in Jackson, Mississippi, with his family. There were so many struggles in the south that Richard decided to leave. So, one day he stole a gun and preserves to sell to buy a ticket to Memphis, Tennessee. Richard hadn't gone any further than the ninth grade, but he dreamed of becoming a writer. It was Memphis where he found a job and borrowed a library card from a white man and began reading. After becoming familiar with the literary community, he moved to Chicago, Illinois.

Living in Chicago was a challenge because he lost his job during the depression. Richard was miserable, so he packed up and moved to New York City. This is where his writing journey began. In 1937, Richard's novel called *Uncle Tom's Children* was published and two years later *Native Son*. It sold 200,000 copies in three weeks. So you see, my brother, Richard didn't give up. He even went on to publish many more wonderful books and was named the finest author in the country.[1]

I can't help but think about how you used to smile when you thought things might get better. But now I see that smile was erased as quickly as it began. I hope you haven't given up because the streets are not the place for you. History tells us that your brother Medgar Evers had to walk twelve miles to school each way just to get an education. After the military, he attended Alcorn A&M College and graduated. After graduation, he joined the NAACP. As the field secretary of this organization, he encouraged black people to exercise their rights to vote. He also worked hard to end segregation in the schools. So, do you ever think that maybe he felt the same way you feel? It's really hard to tell because

Teresa Taylor

he accomplished so much and made a significant difference.[2]

Do you remember that story that you told me when we were talking about you going back to school? I remember you saying that I couldn't possibly understand what it is like living in poverty. When all the food was gone, and there was only one meal per day. Finding a place to sleep was the worst. I remember your eyes watering when you spoke about your father during your childhood. How he subject to bring home things from a nearby dumpster to you and your siblings for Christmas. But wipe those tears my brother because many of us kill our own dreams by giving up. Giving up is hard to do with less and less effort applied. I know that it is hard, but think about your brother Percy Lavon Julian. History tells us that he was born in 1899 in Montgomery, Alabama. He struggled to obtain an education. He was forced to take remedial courses, but graduated with honors and as valedictorian of his class. He went on to study chemistry at Harvard University. He graduated and went to teach at West Virginia State College and Howard University in Washington D.C. He traveled all the way to Vienna, Austria, where he received his doctoral degree and became interested in medical issues. When he returned to the United States, he created synthetic physostigmine, a drug used to treat glaucoma, a disease that causes blindness. Dr. Julian was honored with many awards. His achievements were responsible for saving thousands of lives and reducing the suffering of millions of people, including some who tried to keep him from accomplishing anything.[3]

My brother, I understand the anger you must feel. The tension you have inhaled must be soaring. When I look in your eyes, I see humiliation and grief. It was the same grief once in the eyes of your brother James Baldwin. He was born in 1924 in New York City's Harlem. He spent his time in the library with his white and Jewish friends because they loved reading. James left home at the age of seventeen and began working on his first novel, *Go Tell It on the Mountain*. He felt torn between his loyalties to his community because some laughed at his dream of becoming a writer. But at the same time, his white friends couldn't understand the tension he felt as a black man living in a racist society, so he moved to Paris. Money became a problem, and he became hungry and broke. He sold his clothes and typewriter. After that, things became better because he was accepted by the French. This gave him an opportunity to write.

In 1955, he heard of the vicious murder of Emmett Till. This news had a huge impact on James. Angry but hopeful, James wrote many essays and novels of the life he lived and the things he saw during this time. He wrote, "We, the black and white, deeply need each other here if we are really to become a nation. If we really want, that is, to achieve our identity, our maturity, as men and women."

You see, my brother, the anger you must feel is expected but not justified. In spite of the inequity, hope, perseverance and self-esteem overcame your brothers. It definitely overcame your brother Thurgood Marshall. He was born in Baltimore in 1908. He constantly got into trouble in school. As punishment, the principal would make him memorize sections of the U.S. Constitution. He graduated with honors from Lincoln University in Pennsylvania. Later he attended Harvard University Law School, specializing in civil rights cases. In 1954, Marshall was challenged with a case called *Brown v. The Board of Education of Topeka, Kansas*. He argued that segregation concluded that black children were not as good as white children. It placed black children at a disadvantage. The court agreed. He was the first black man

Teresa Taylor

to serve as the associate justice of the Supreme Court in 1967. He translated the words *Equal Justice Under Law* into reality.[4]

My brother, I hope you're not still feeling hopeless. From our conversation, I know that you have dreams because you've talked about them. I can remember the excitement you felt when talking about all the things you wanted to accomplish. I know you have dreams just as your brother Dr. Martin Luther King Jr. did. Can you remember what his dream was? He only wanted equal rights for everyone. Most people dream of having a nice big home, a car and lots of money, but he wanted this and many other opportunities for all people. But his first priority was black people. He was born in Atlanta Georgia, on January 15, 1929. With his parents being highly respected in the community, Martin had a chance at a descent life, one would think, but this was far from the truth. There were many violent and racist white people at that time, and Martin was against violence. After attending theological seminary to become a minister like his father, Martin was sure he was ready to make a change in the world. His decision to do just that changed many injustices in the world for good. President Kennedy was working on a civil rights bill, and this launched 250,000 people to Washington D.C. to support the speeches of Martin and many others. This gathering made a change but didn't end the civil rights movement. White men covered in sheets called themselves the Ku Klux Klan, and they were angry and jealous about this. They decided to bomb the Sixteenth Baptist Church in Birmingham, which killed four little black girls.[5]

The 1964 Civil Rights Act ended segregation in public places, so the boycotts and marches were not in vain. Martin had many other things to do after this. Mississippi was the worst place, having voting problems. So, the civil rights groups set up a Summer Project Group to help encourage blacks to register as voters. On June 21, three CORE workers were sent to help, but Michael Schwerner, James Chaney, and Andrew Goodman were murdered by the Klan. In 1965, Congress signed a bill called the Voting Rights Bill. This guaranteed black people voting rights. Martin was so against violence that he spoke out against the Vietnam War. This turned President Johnson, who was once for Martin, against him. But this didn't change Martin's mind about nonviolence and equal rights. On April 4, 1968, Martin was killed. James Earl Ray ended Martin's last breath. Martin's speech and dream was this and many others: "I have a dream that even one day the state of Mississippi, a desert state sweltering with the heat of injustice and oppression, will be transformed into as oasis of freedom and justice."[6]

My brother, many of your people were conscious of the changes needed at this time but were afraid to take on the task of the world. You must change your way of thinking. When all odds are against you, you are the one to step out there on that limb all by yourself. You are your own ammunition. This is what your brother Malcolm X did. He wasn't as nonviolent as Martin at first, but many things changed him. He started his life on the streets doing illegal things. He was sent to jail for six years for burglary. In prison he met with a man who believed in a religious group called the Nation of Islam. Then it was led by Elijah Muhammad. They promoted independence for black people. Malcolm spent twelve years organizing and spreading the word of the Muslims. He definitely condemned the nonviolent efforts that he civil rights movement wanted to achieve. He felt that progress was too slow, and many angry black people felt the same, so they followed Malcolm. Malcolm was such an eloquent speaker that many in the Nation became jealous of him. In December 1963, Malcolm left the Nation of Islam. Elijah Muhammad suspended him. This didn't stop Malcolm from forming his own organization, called the Organization of Afro American Unity (OAAU). On February 21, Malcolm was shot and killed. Three men from the Nation of Islam were convicted of murder. Malcolm said, "We have to keep in mind at all times that we are not fighting for integration, nor are we fighting for separation. We are fighting for recognition as free humans in this society."[7]

So you see, my brother, Malcolm X decided to step out there on that limb by himself and become an individual, but was killed because of it. Times are a lot different now, and you have an opportunity to step out there and not be killed for it. You are a human being, and it's time you stood up for who you are and what you can be. I have to tell you about your brother Jesse Jackson. He believes that you are somebody. "I am somebody!" Jesse believed in this slogan from his heart. He was born in Greenville, South Carolina. He received a football scholarship to attend college at the University of Illinois. After he received his B.A., he attended theological seminary and continued his involvement in the civil rights movement. In 1965, he met with Dr. Martin Luther King Jr. at the Selma march and became a member of the SCLC. He later returned to Chicago to help Dr. King prepare for his "Campaign to End Slums" in Chicago. Jesse ran for president twice and surprisingly had many supporters, but not enough to win. He made a stand for what he believed, which was that he is some body, and so are you.[8]

My brother, I didn't mean to take up much of your time, and I know that I am persistent, overprotective and always on the defensive for you. But there is no one like you, and I love you with all my heart. I know what you are thinking right now. You are thinking that you have to do things this way because you have to feel like somebody even if it hurts your family. I am your sista, and I feel the same way sometimes, but I know when there is time for a change. The time is now, my brother. I want to remind you of your brother Barack Obama. Did you hear anything in the neighborhood about him running for president? If you did, it is true. All the family and friends are shining with smiles. We are supporting him until the end. Barack is a remarkable, intelligent, calm and well-spoken man. You should see the way he gets his message across. He attended Harvard University and became senator; although that's a great accomplishment, he hasn't stopped. He just became president. My brother, I know you are smiling right now because that's the real you. I know you want to clean up your life and start all over. Well, with all I have written about the accomplishments your brothers have made, I hope this encourages you to understand that it is possible for any dream to come true. Even when you are a day late and a dollar short. Even when you have to rob Peter to pay Paul. And even when your pockets are empty but your dream is full. We have to help each other, my brother, because of the younger brothers and sisters. They need to know that we've got their back, no matter what. They need to know without a doubt that making something of their lives is well worth the struggles.

I know you don't know where your ending point lies, but it will be good to know that you tried and experienced many good things that were promised you before the ending time. So, my brother, I can see you now smiling and standing on your feet preparing for the next phase of your most precious life. I'll be here waiting for you and hoping that once you've walked away, you won't look back. I know you are probably waiting for the mailman, but this time you have received a letter. It's only your sista reaching out to you

Teresa Taylor

because you seem to have forgotten who I am. Many times you have referred to me as a b—- or a wh—-, but I know it was mistaken identity. The sun will shine in your life, and as you grow, others will take root and spread the most beautiful change in the world.

Sincerely,

Your sista

P.S. I love you, my brother. Whenever the storm is near, take shelter, but when love is near, grab hold.

Notes

[1] Susan Altman, *Extraordinary Black Americans*

[2] Ibid.

[3] Ibid.

[4] Ibid.

[5] Ibid.

[6] Ibid.

[7] Ibid.

[8] Ibid.